THE POETICAL MANUSCRIPTS

OF MARK AKENSIDE

C Pond pinx.t 1754.

E Fisher Sculp.t 1772.

MARK AKENSIDE

ÆTATIS XXXV.

THE POETICAL MANUSCRIPTS

OF

MARK AKENSIDE

IN THE

RALPH M. WILLIAMS COLLECTION
AMHERST COLLEGE LIBRARY

REPRODUCED IN FACSIMILE

WITH AN

INTRODUCTION BY ROBIN C. DIX

AMHERST COLLEGE PRESS · AMHERST, MASSACHUSETTS · 1988

Publication of this work was made possible by The Friends of The Amherst College Library and the Howard A. Newton '06 Memorial Fund.

The frontispiece is reproduced from that in Jeremiah Dyson's copy of *The Poems of Mark Akenside*, 1772. All reproductions are actual size, unless otherwise noted.

Library of Congress Cataloging in Publication Data

Akenside, Mark, 1721–1770.
　The poetical manuscripts of Mark Akenside in the
Ralph M. Williams Collection, Amherst College Library.

　1. Akenside, Mark, 1721–1770—Manuscripts—
Facsimiles.　2. Manuscripts, English—Facsimiles.
I. Amherst College Library.　II. Title.
PR3311.D59 1988　　821'.6　　88–6200
ISBN 0-943184-02-9

Printed in the United States of America by Meriden-Stinehour Press.

INTRODUCTION

THE POETRY of Mark Akenside (1721–1770) may not be widely read today, but in the eighteenth century and for much of the nineteenth his work was held in the very highest esteem, and writers as eminent as Wordsworth and Coleridge were considerably indebted to him. In 1772, two years after his death, his friend and patron Jeremiah Dyson brought out *The Poems of Mark Akenside, M.D.* in both quarto and octavo editions. This volume contained the vast majority of Akenside's poetic output, including his most important and influential work, *The Pleasures of Imagination* (1744), and a substantial fragment—2,100 lines—of an almost entirely rewritten version with the slightly altered title *The Pleasures of the Imagination*.

The Amherst Akenside holdings were originally mounted in Dyson's own copy of the 1772 *Poems*,[1] and together they form the largest single collection of his poetic manuscripts in the world. Of the four pieces in the poet's own hand, the two earliest seem to be "Ode to a gentleman whose mistress had married an old man" and "Ode to a gentleman in hazard of falling in love". These works were first published in *Odes on Several Subjects* (1745); they subsequently reappeared in heavily revised form in the second edition of that collection (1760), and again, with yet further revisions, in the posthumous *Poems* edited by Dyson. The manuscripts give the pieces in a state quite different from that of the first printed texts, and almost certainly earlier. Their relationship with the first published edition is clearly closer than with any of the subsequent versions, since when they agree with only one of the printed texts, the text in question is the 1745 edition of the odes. But there are also a number of instances where the manuscripts offer a reading that does not appear in print at all—implying either that they predate the published versions, or that Akenside made an emendation which he subsequently deleted. In "Ode to a gentleman in hazard of falling in love" there are two cases where the unique reading continues for a whole stanza; and while the manuscript of "Ode to a gentleman whose mistress had married an old man" does not contain any unique readings on quite this scale, it differs metrically from all published versions in having a pentameter instead of a tetrameter for the final line of each stanza. Textual evidence, then, enables us to ascribe these manuscripts to some time before 1745 with reasonable confidence, and the handwriting provides further corroborative evidence: this is Akenside's early "fair copy" style, and compares with, say, his very carefully written letter of 1742 to the Rev. Mr. Barker.[2]

"The Complaint", also in Akenside's neatest hand, was not published until Dyson's 1772 edition of the *Poems*, where it appears as XIV in the second book of odes. The text of the manuscript differs in only a few minor details from the printed version. Again it is not possible to date the document precisely, but the word "squandèrer" (stanza 3) perhaps offers a clue: the unusual method of indicating elision by placing an apostrophe over the letter to be elided first occurs in a dated manuscript in January 1749 Old Series (i.e. January 1750). The manuscript in question, "Ode to Sir Francis-Henry Drake, Barᵗ. January M.DCC.XLIX. O.S.", is also in the Amherst collection. Perhaps because of the various references to personal friends in the work, neither Akenside nor Dyson chose to publish it, and it did not appear in print until 1942.[3] The handwriting,

---

1. They have been removed in order better to preserve them.

2. British Library MS. Add. 21,508, f. 26.
3. See R. M. Williams, "Two Unpublished Poems by Mark Akenside", *Modern Language Notes* 57 (1942), 626–631. This work is not to be confused with a second ode to Drake which did appear in the 1772 *Poems* (XII in the first book

while superficially very different from that in the other autograph manuscripts at Amherst, is typical of Akenside's later, and faster, hand.

This later style is in many ways similar to Dyson's hand, which is exemplified in the manuscript of "Epode". Close examination, however, reveals several distinctive features, and comparison with autograph letters preserved in other libraries places beyond doubt R. M. Williams' ascription of this manuscript to Dyson.[4] "Epode", the second of the poems published in 1942 by Williams, represents one stage in the long controversy between Akenside and William Warburton, the quarrelsome cleric and critic. The prose material in Akenside's hand at Amherst also relates to this feud. In one of his major works, *The Divine Legation of Moses* (2 vols., London, 1738–1741), Warburton had argued strongly against Shaftesbury's theory that it is impossible to ridicule things that are good, true and beautiful, and that susceptibility to ridicule can therefore be used as a test of truth. Akenside had nevertheless incorporated Shaftesbury's theory into *The Pleasures of Imagination* (1744), and had in places expressed himself in such a way that Warburton believed he was being attacked in turn. He therefore pilloried Akenside in the preface to another of his works, *Remarks on Several Occasional Reflections* (1744). A defence of Akenside, written either by the poet himself or by Dyson, appeared shortly afterwards, entitled *An Epistle to the Rev. Mr. Warburton, occasioned by his Treatment of the Author of the Pleasures of Imagination*. This put an end to open hostilities for a time, although beneath the surface the bad feeling rumbled on: for example, Warburton tried to contribute to *The Museum*, a periodical published by Robert Dodsley, but his material was rejected—presumably because Akenside was editing the publication. In 1766, however, the contro-versy erupted again. Warburton published a fifth edition of *The Divine Legation of Moses*, and at the end of his ironic dedication "To the Free-Thinkers" he reprinted (with a few minor revisions) his 1744 attack on Akenside from *Remarks on Several Occasional Reflections*. Akenside retaliated by publishing a poem he had written in 1751—*An Ode to the late Thomas Edwards, Esq*. This was a two-pronged attack on Warburton: first, Edwards had taken issue with the principles underlying his edition of Shakespeare in a work called *The Canons of Criticism*, so that any expression of solidarity with Edwards was an implied affront to Warburton; and secondly, Akenside referred in a footnote to an old letter he had found from Warburton to Pope's enemy Matthew Concanen. This was particularly embarrassing, as Warburton had later edited Pope and defended him against his many detractors. The letter to Concanen at Amherst is Akenside's transcript of the original document, while the account of a conversation with Richard Palmer on May 4, 1766 contains further evidence of Warburton's intimacy with "Theobald & his confederates"—among whom, of course, was Concanen.

The poem "Occasion'd by Dr. Johnson's 'Life of Akenside'", although it is signed "J.D.", cannot be by Akenside's friend and patron: he had died in 1776, while Johnson's "Life" did not appear until 1781. The hand is in any case quite different from the hand of "Epode". The verses were probably written by Dyson's son, also Jeremiah Dyson. Finally, the transcripts in an unknown hand from *The Pleasures of the Imagination*[5]—the incomplete, rewritten version of the 1744 poem—are of interest because of the word "undivided" (513). The published text reads "uncorrupted". It is not clear whether the writer was influenced by the occurrence of "undivided" earlier in the printed version (494), or whether he was transcribing a manuscript which actually contained a different reading here.

ROBIN C. DIX

of odes). The manuscript of this second Drake ode has been discovered by Harriet Jump, who describes it and discusses its contents in "Two New Akenside Manuscripts", *Review of English Studies* (forthcoming May 1988).

4. I am most grateful to Mr Hilton Kelliher of the Department of Western Manuscripts, British Library, for his expert analysis of the hands in question, and his resulting confirmation of R. M. Williams' ascriptions.

5. Book I, lines 489–491 and 509–515.

The Ralph M. Williams Collection

RALPH MEHLIN WILLIAMS, a graduate of Amherst College in the Class of 1933, took his doctorate at Yale University in 1938. (He had studied for one year at the University of Cambridge, England, before coming to Amherst, where his father was Professor of Physics.) At Yale, he studied with—among others—Wilmarth S. Lewis, and conceived thereby an interest in eighteenth-century English culture and literature that lasted throughout his lifetime, and guided the formation of his collection of books and manuscripts, as well as a major part of his scholarly career.

His first book, *Private Charity in England, 1747–1757*, was produced in collaboration with Lewis, and appeared in 1938. He also worked with Lewis as editor of volume 15 of the Yale Edition of the Correspondence of Horace Walpole, *Horace Walpole's Correspondence with Henry Zouch* (1951).

But his life of John Dyer, *Poet, Painter, and Parson* (New York, 1956) touches closer to the heart of his collecting, which focussed on the works of Akenside, of Dyer, and of James Thomson. The collection as it now stands includes virtually all variants of the works of those three men published in the eighteenth century (and many later editions of *The Seasons*, which offer a conspectus of typographical taste through two centuries), as well as related eighteenth-century publications and select manuscript material.

In addition to the Akenside manuscripts reproduced here, Professor Williams acquired (and published, in 1955 in *Modern Language Notes*) a manuscript of a previously unknown poem by Thomson, "An Ode on the Winter Solstice," now in the collection at Amherst.

The manuscript of John Dyer's letter of 7 March 1752 to Thomas Edwards now in the collection was not acquired by Professor Williams, but it exemplifies the continuing life of the collection: Its purchase was enabled by an endowment he created which, though modest in size, supports regular additions to and expansion of the collection. The Ralph M. Williams Collection is thus not only the centerpiece of Amherst's eighteenth-century English holdings, but a living and growing memorial, enabling current and future generations of Amherst students to share in his enthusiasm.

JOHN LANCASTER
Curator of Special Collections
Amherst College Library

Ode
to a gentleman in hazard of falling
in love.

No! foolish boy — To virtuous fame
If now thy early hopes be vow'd,
If true ambition's nobler flame
Command thy footsteps from the croud,
Lean not to love's inchanting snare,
His dances, his delights beware,
Nor mingle in the band of young & fair.

By thought, by dangers & by toils
The wreath of just renown is worn;
Nor will ambition's awful spoils
The flow'ry pomp of ease adorn:
But love dissolves the nerve of thought,
By love unmanly fears are taught,
And love's reward with slothful arts is bought.

Say'st thou thy heart is warn'd of this?
And not for love's fond hope inclines
To taste the cool refining bliss
Where beauty in thy converse joins?
O rebel fit for love to tame!
And blind to man's relenting frame,
O bliss in beauty cool from passion's flame!

But

Akenside MS 1, fo. 1r. "Ode to a gentleman in hazard of falling in love." Before 1745.

2

But if, intire from passion's pow'r,
Such bliss be all thy heart intends,
Go where the white-wing'd evening-hour
On Delia's vernal walk descends;
Go! while the pleasing, peaceful scene
Becomes her voice, becomes her mien,
Sweet as her smiles & as her brow serene.

Attend while that harmonious tongue
Each bosom, each desire commands;
Apollo's lute by Hermes strung,
And touch'd by chast Minerva's hands,
Attend — I feel a force divine,
O Delia form my pow'rs to thine,
That half thy graces seem already mine.

Yet conscious of the dangerous charm,
Soon let me turn my steps away;
Nor oft provoke the lovely harm,
Nor once relax my reason's sway.
But thou, my friend — what sudden sighs!
What means the blush that comes & flies?
Why stop? why speechless? why revert thy eyes?

So soon again to meet the fair?
So absent all this parting hour?
— O yet, unlucky youth, beware,
While yet to think is in thy pow'r.
In vain, with friendship's flatt'ring name,
Thy passion masks its inward shame;
Friendship! the treach'rous fuel of thy flame.

Once

3

Once, I remember, tir'd of love,
I spurn'd his hard tyrannic ~~mumur~~ chain,
Yet won the ~~mumur~~ haughty fair to prove
What sober joys with friendship reign:
No more I sigh'd, complain'd or swore;
The nymph's coy arts appear'd no more;
But each could laugh at what we felt before.

Well-pleas'd we pass'd the chearful day,
To unreserv'd discourse resign'd,
And I inchanted to survey
One generous woman's real mind;
But soon I wonder'd what possess'd
Each wakeful night my anxious breast,
No other friendship e'er had broke my rest!

— Fool that I was! — And now e'in now
While thus I preach the Stoic strain,
Unless I ~~huddly~~ from Laura's view,
An hour unsays it all again:
— Oh! friend, when love directs her eyes
To pierce where every passion lies,
Where is the ~~wounds~~ the cautious, or the wise?
firm,

Akenside MS 1, fo. 2r.

Ode

to a gentleman whose mistress had married
an old man.

Indeed, my S——n, if to find
That gold a female's vow can gain,
If this had e'er disturb'd your mind,
Or cost one serious moment's pain,
I should have said the pompous rules
You learnt of moralists & schools,
Were very useless all & very vain.

Yet I perhaps mistake the case;
And tho' with this heroic air,
Like one that holds a nobler chace,
You seem the lady's loss to bear,
Perhaps your heart belied your tongue,
And thinks my censure mighty wrong,
~~Without~~ count it such a slight affair.
(To laugh &)
                                    When

Akenside MS 2, fo. *1*ʳ. "Ode to a gentleman whose mistress had married
an old man." Before 1745.

When Hesper gilds the shaded sky,
Slow-wandring thro' the well-known grove,
Methinks I see you cast your eye
Back to the morning scenes of love;
Her tender look, her graceful way,
The sprightly things you heard her say,
With sweet distress your struggling fancy move.

Then tell me, is your soul intire?
Does wisdom calmly hold her throne?
Then can you question each desire?
Bid this remain, & that begone?
No tear swift-starting from your eye?
No kindling blush you know not why?
No stealing sigh, no faintly-stifled groan?

Away with this unmanly mood!
See where the hoary churl appears,
Whose hand hath seiz'd the favrite good
Which you reserv'd for happier years;

While

Akenside MS 2, fo. 1v.

3

While side by side the blushing maid
Shrinks from his visage, half afraid,
Spite of the false, the sickly joy she wears.

Ye guardian pow'rs of love & fame,
This chast harmonious pair behold,
And thus reward the generous flame
Of all who barter vows for gold.
O bloom of youth & tender charms
Well buried in a dotard's arms!
O worthy price of beauty to be sold!

Cease then to gaze unthankful boy;
Let, let her go, the venal fair;
Unworthy She to give you joy!
Then wherefore should she give you care?
Lay, lay your myrtle garland down,
And let the willow's virgin-crown
With whiter omens bind your happy hair.

O

Akenside MS 2, fo. 2r.

4

O just escap'd the faithless main,
Tho' driv'n unwilling on the land!
To guide your favour'd steps again,
Behold your better Genius stand:
Where Plato's olive courts your eye,
Where Hamden's laurel blooms on high,
Behold! he lifts his heav'n-directed hand.

When these are blended on your brow
The willow will be scorn'd no more;
Or if that love-forsaken bough
The pitying, laughing girls deplore,
Yet still shall I most freely swear,
Your dress has much a better air
Than all that ever beau or bridegroom wore.

Akenside MS 2, fo. 2ᵛ.

Ode
to Sir Francis-Henry Drake, Bar.t
January, M.DCC.XLIX. O.S.

1.

While by the order of the day,
Next week, the House & Speaker pray
That heaven may néer, at Britain's hand,
The royal martyr's life demand;
While Bentham labours much in vain
The rights of freedom to maintain
With good Saint Charles's blessed reign;

2.

Then, Drake, to Hampstead haste away,
Where Dyson spends with me the day:
And try if Hardinge cannot find
That fate hath just one more design'd:
Townshend is digging at his farm;
Nor would a loud promiscuous swarm
Or thee, or any of us charm.

3. I

Akenside MS 3, fo. 1ʳ. "Ode to Sir Francis-Henry Drake, Barᵗ. January, M.DCC.XLIX. O.S." January 1750.

3.

I hate the table & the treat
Where friends, beset with strangers, meet;
Where prudent form the tongue restrains
From utt'ring what the heart contains;
While, in your own despite, your eyes
Tell how importantly you prize
The deep discourse which round you flies.

4.

But say; from orators ador'd,
From every heir to every board,
From Egmont's pathos, Warren's flights,
And Nugent's tragi-comic flights,
Can'st thou an hour's attention steal
To talk with me of England's weal,
And smile at my untutor'd zeal?

5.

Then, if too grave the subject grow,
(Foreboding aught we fear to know)
To bring more pleasing prospects home,
Thro' distant ages we can roam;
When Athens spurn'd the Persian chain;
When thy fam'd grandsire aw'd the main,
Or Somers guided William's reign.

6. Thence

Akenside MS 3, fo. 1v.

6.

Thence may we turn to calmer views,
The haunts of science & the Muse;
To groves where Milton walks alone,
To Bacon's philosophic throne;
Or where those Attic themes we find,
The moral law, the' almighty mind,
And man for future worlds design'd.

7.

O Drake, in spite of all the zeal
Which for the public oft we feel,
When I before the shrine of fame
Present some English patriot's name,
Or when thy nobler cares demand
How England's Genius safe may stand
From usury's insatiate hand;

8.

Yet, if blind selfishness can *foil
Both Barnard's hope & Pelham's toil,
Surely the happiest hours below,
(Which yet must from the public flow)
The hours, which most sincerely please,
Belong to private scenes like these,
To friendship & to letter'd ease.

---

* the attempts to defeat the reduction of the
interest of the national debt.

Ode.
The Complaint.

I.

Away! away!
Tempt me no more, insidious love:
Thy soothing sway
Long did my youthful bosom prove:
At length thy treason i discern'd,
At length some dear-bought caution earn'd:
Away! nor hope my riper age to move.

II.

I know, i see
Her merit. Needs it now be shown,
Alass, to me?
How often, to myself unknown,
The graceful, gentle, virtuous maid
Have i admir'd! how often said,
What joy, to call a heart like her's one's own!

III.

But flattering god,
O spendthrift of content & ease,
~~Thou that ~~
Squanderer
In thy abode
I will   lesson   learn
This care's rude menace ~~~~~~~ to please?
O! say, deceiver, hast thou won
Proud fortune to attend thy throne,
Or plac'd thy friends above her stern decrees?

Akenside MS 4, fo. 1r. "Ode. The Complaint." Ca. 1750?

Epode.

O parent of the Muses, who alone,
From Time's destructive might, hast pow'r to save
The works of man; O Memory, behold
This votive tablet, which the faithful hand
Of Cleophron suspends amid thy dome.
Accept the gift propitious; & preserve
The record which it holds, the voice & prayer
Of jealous fame. For by ignoble feet
Soon will thy courts be trampled, & the tongues
Of Hippias & Thrax with sland'rous rites
Affront thy altar. But permit not thou,
O queen, their unblest envy to impair
Thy servant's name; or from his duteous cares
To turn thy gracious notice. Long their arts,
Their snares distributed thro' vulgar paths,
Neglecting hath he scorn'd; secure of thee,
Secure that never thine eternal gates
The rude access of ignorance & rage
Would suffer. But behold; the favour'd bard
Who lately this heroic mansion trod,
Thy priest, with evil auspices to them
                                    Hath

Akenside MS 5, fo. 1r. "Epode." In the hand of the elder Jeremiah Dyson.

Hath left the charge his offrings to present
Before thy footstool. Fierce with his commands,
Ev'n now presumptuous up thy awful heights
They come; with mutual flattery sounding forth
That honour much unhop'd; & fell revenge
To each gainsayer, & envenom'd wounds
To all who spurn'd erewhile their sordid toils,
Denouncing. But, immortal matron, say;
Wilt thou accept them? wilt thou stoop to hear
The worship of blasphemers? No. by all
The sacred Manes dearest to thy reign,
By all the praise of sages, patriots, kings,
Dash their foul homage; & let equal shame
Repay the profanation. So well-pleas'd
Shall purer votaries, throughout the bounds
Of Albion's land, to thy asserted throne
Do rev'rence. So shall my devoted song
Nor day nor night refuse to deck thy shrine
With trophies won from envy & from death.

In the possession of Dr Hardinge

Dear Sir

     having had no more regard for those papers which I spoke of & promised to Mr Theobald, than just what they deserv'd I in vain sought for them thro' a number of loose papers that had the same kind of abortive birth. I used to make it one good part of my amusement in reading the English poets, those of them I mean whose vein flows regularly & constantly, as well as clearly, to trace them to their sources; & observe what oar, as well as what sleime & gravel they brought down with them. Dryden I observe borrows for want of leasure, & Pope for want of Genius: Milton out of pride, & Addison out of modesty. And now I speak of this latter, that you & Mr Theobald may see of what kind these Idle collections are, & likewise to give you my notion of what we may safely pronounce an imitation, for it is not I presume the same train of ideas that follow in the same description of an Antient & a modern, where nature when attended to, always supplys the same stores, which will autorize us to pro-nounce the latter an imitation. for the most judicious of all poets, Terence, has observ'd of his own science _Nihil est dictum, quod non sit dictum prius_: For these reasons, I say I give myself the pleasure of setting down some imitations I observ'd in the _Cato_ of Addison.

Addison.   A day, an hour of virtuous liberty
        Is worth a whole eternity in bondage. _Act. 2. Sc. 1._

Tully. Quod si immortalitas consequeretur præsentis periculi
       fugam, tamen eo magis ea fugenda esse videretur, quo
       diuturnior esset servitus. _Philipp. Or. 10.ª_

Addison. Bid him disband his legions
       Restore the Commonwealth to Liberty
       Submit his actions to the public censure,
       And stand the Judgement of a Roman Senate
       Bid him do this & Cato is his friend.   _Sc. 2._

Tully. Pacem vult? arma deponat, roget, deprecetur. Neminem
       equiorem reperiet quam me.   _Philipp. 5.ª_

                            _Ad-_

Akenside MS 6, fo. _1ʳ_. Transcript, dated 29 April 1766, by Akenside of a letter from William Warburton to Matthew Concanen, 2 January 1726.

Addison.   (2)   But what is life?
       'Tis not to stalk about & draw fresh air
       From time to time ——
       'Tis to be free. When Liberty is gone
       Life grows insipid & has lost its Relish.   Sc. 3.

Tully. Non enim in spiritu vita est: sed ea nulla est omnino
      servienti.   Philipp. 10ª

Addison.   Remember o my friends the laws the rights
       The gen'rous plan of power deliver'd down
       From age to age by your renowned forefathers.
       O never let it perish in your hands.   Act 3. Sc. 5.

Tully. —— Hanc [libertatem scilt] retinete, quæso, Quirites,
      quam vobis, tanquam hereditatem majores nostri reliquerunt.
                                 (Philipp. 4ª

Addison.   The mistress of the world, the seat of Empire,
       The nurse of Heros the Delight of Gods.

Tully.   Roma domus virtutis, imperii, dignitatis, domicilium
      gloriæ, lux orbis terrarum.   de oratore.

The first half of the 5 Sc. 3. Act. is nothing but a transcript from
the 9ᵗ book of lucan between the 300 & the 700ᵗʰ line.
You see by this specimen the exactness of Mr Addison's judgement
who wanting sentiments worthy the Roman Cato sought for them
in Tully & Lucan. When he wou'd give his subject those terrible graces
which Dion: Hallicar: complains he cou'd find no where but in
Homer, he takes the assistance of our Shakespear, who in his
Julius Cæsar has painted the Conspirators with a pomp & terrour
that perfectly astonishes. hear our British Homer.
       Between the acting of a dreadful thing
       And the first motion, all the Intrim is
       Like a phantasma or a hideous dream
       The Genius & the mortal Instruments
       Are then in Council, & the state of Man
       Like to a little Kingdom, suffers then
       The nature of an insurrection.
Mr Addison has thus imitated it.
       O think what anxious moments pass between
                            The

(3.)

The birth of plots, & their last fatal periods
O 'tis a dreadful interval of time,
Filled up with horror all, & big with death.

I have two things to observe on this imitation. 1. the decorum
this exact Mr of propriety has observed. In the Conspiracy of
Shakespears discription, the fortunes of Cesar & the roman Empire
were concern'd. And the magnificent circumstances of
     " The Genius & the mortal instruments
     " Are then in council.
is exactly proportioned to the dignity of the subject. But this wou'd
have been too great an apparatus to the desertion of Syphax & the
rape of Sempronius, & therefore Mr Addison omits it. II. The other
thing more worth our notice is that Mr A. was so greatly moved
& affected with the pomp of Sh: description that instead of co-
pying his Authors sentiments, he has before he was aware given
us only the marks of his own impressions on the reading him. For

     " O 'tis a dreadful interval of time
     " Filled up with horror all, & big with death.
are but the affections rais'd by such lively images as these
     ———— " All the Interim is
     " Like a Phantasma or a hideous dream.
                    &
     " The State of Man — like to a little kingdom suffers then
               " The nature of an insurrection.
Again when Mr Addison wou'd paint the softer passions he has
recourse to Lee who certainly had a peculiar genius that way.
thus his Juba
     " True, she is fair. O how divinely fair!
coldly imitates Lee in his Alex:
     " Then he wou'd talk: Good Gods how he wou'd talk!
I pronounce the more boldly of this, because Mr A: in his 39 Spec:
expresses his admiration of it. My paper fails me, or I shou'd
now offer to Mr Theobald an objection agt Shakespear acquaintance
with the antients. As it appears to me of great weight, & as it is
necessary he shou'd be prepared to obviate all that occur on that
head. But some other opportunity will present itselfe. You
may now, Sr justly complain of my ill manners in deferring
                                                    till

Akenside MS 6, fo. 2r.

(4)

till now, what should have been first of all acknowledged due to
you. which is my thanks for all your favours when in town. par-
-ticularly for introducing me to the knowledge of those worthy
& most ingenious Gentlemen that made up our last nights
conversation. I am, Sir with all esteem your most obliged
friend & humble servant   W. Warburton.
                    Newarke Jan. 2. 1726

        The superscription is thus:

For
    Mr M. Concanen at
    Mr Woodwards at the
    half moon in ffleetstreet
                London.

_____

This letter was found about the year 1750, by Dr Gawin
Knight, first librarian to the British Museum, in fitting
up a house which he had taken in Crane Court, Fleetstreet.
The house had, for a long time before, been let in lodgings;
&, in all probability, Concanen had lodged there. The ori-
-ginal letter has been many years in my possession, & is
here most exactly copied, with its several little inaccuracies
in grammar, spelling, & punctuation.

        April 29, 1768.   MAkenside.

_____

P. 344

Akenside MS 6, fo. 2ᵛ.

vide the last page, note on St. v. of X ode – B. 11

On Sunday Evening, May 4, 1766, M.r Rich-
-ard Palmer, Chaplain to Sir John Cust,
Speaker to the House of Commons, being
with several other gentlemen at the Bishop
of Lincoln's in Scotland-Yard, & the conversa
-tion turning on a charge which had been lately
brought in print against D.r Warburton, Bish-
-op of Gloucester, that he had been deeply ingag'd with
Theobald & his confederates in their enmity
against M.r Pope; M.r Palmer mention'd of his own know-
-ledge that M.r Warburton us'd to be very vehe
-ment in conversation against the Essay on
Man; & that in a club at Grantham, of which
himself & M.r Warburton were members, the
latter us'd to threaten that he would write a-
-gainst it & shew it to be made up of fatalism
& Spinosism: but M.r Smith, another member
of the club, dissuaded him from doing so, by rea-
-son of M.r Pope's great authority in the world.
Which advice, added M.r Palmer, M.r Warburton
so far follow'd that, instead of writing against
the essay on man, he wrote in defence of it
against from that very accusation.
(This I was assur'd of by D.r Heberden, D.r Ross & M.r Maudiut
who were present & heard M.r Palmer's narrative.)

Akenside MS 7, fo. 1r. Akenside's account of a conversation with Richard Palmer, 4 May 1766.

Occasion'd by Dr. Johnson's "Life of Akenside".

O Akenside, where'er thy Harp is hung,
Whether with Pindar's on some ~~venturous~~ awful height,
Or in the ~~Elysian~~ laureate *✗ shades which more delight
Harmonious Virgil; let no Censor's Tongue

Affront its Guardian Spirit, Fame has flung
~~Around~~ Before thy honour'd name her ample shield
'Gainst which in vain, by strange Ambition stung
Rude Pedantry his barbarous force shall weild:

For deem it ~~~~ ought of wonder ~~~~ that the hand
Which aims at Lyttleton the ~~~~ unworthy blow
(Foe in her purest forms to Liberty)
Which Gray's ~~~~ impressive impulse ~~could~~ can withstand
And envious shades o'er Milton's splendor throw
Should strive to tear the hallow'd wreath from thee.

J.D.

✗ See Pleasures of
Imagination.
Book. 1. l. 5a

Akenside MS 8, fo. *1*ʳ. Transcript, in an unidentified hand, of Book I, lines 489–491 and 509–515 of *The Pleasures of the Imagination*.

Opposite: "Occasion'd by Dʳ. Johnson's 'Life of Akenside'." Presumably by the younger Jeremiah Dyson. After 1781. (Written on the verso of the title-leaf of Dyson's copy of *The Poems of Mark Akenside*, 1772. Reproduced at 90% original size.)